This journal belongs to:

Published by Christian Art Publishers
PO Box 1599, Vereeniging, 1930, RSA

© 2019
First edition 2019

Designed by Christian Art Publishers

Images used under license from Shutterstock.com

Printed in China

ISBN 978-1-4321-3075-6

21 22 23 24 25 26 27 28 29 30 – 18 17 16 15 14 13 12 11 10 9

My PRAYER Journal

120 days of prayer,
reflection and praise

CHRISTIAN ART
PUBLISHERS

How to Pray

Matthew 6:9-13

Praise God for who He is
and what He has done.

Our Father in heaven, hallowed be Your name.

Repent of sins I have committed.

*And forgive us our debts, as we also have
forgiven our debtors.*

Ask for the needs of others and for my needs.

*Give us today our daily bread.
And lead us not into temptation, but deliver us
from the evil one.*

Yield my will to God's will. Change my plans
to God's plans for me.

*Your kingdom come, Your will be done,
on earth as it is in heaven.*

The ACTS Way to Pray

Adoration >>> Tell God how wonderful He is and worship Him.

Confession >>> Admit your sins and ask for forgiveness.

Thanksgiving >>> Tell God how grateful you are for what He has done in your life.

Supplication >>> Make requests to God - for yourself and for others.

Date: March 2, 2022

Prayer does not change God, but it changes him who prays. ~ Søren Kierkegaard

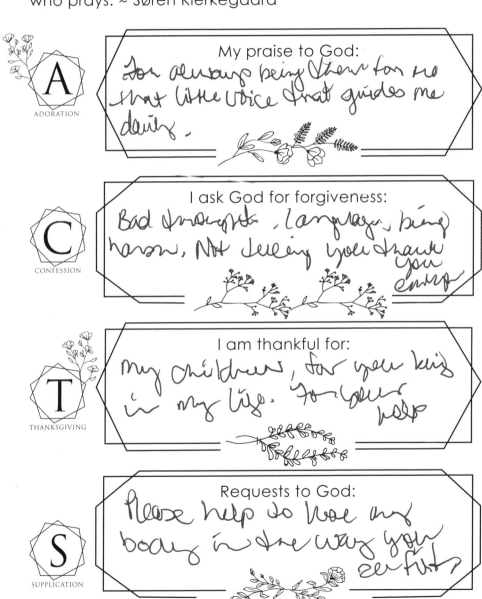

A — ADORATION

My praise to God:

For always being there for me that little voice that guides me daily.

C — CONFESSION

I ask God for forgiveness:

Bad thoughts, language, being harsh, Not telling you thank you enough

T — THANKSGIVING

I am thankful for:

My children, for your being in my life. For your help

S — SUPPLICATION

Requests to God:

Please help to lose my body in the way you see fits

Date: March 13, 2022

Verse for today:

Be completely patient, humble and gentle, bearing one another with love.

Prayers for others:

I pray that you lift little Mathew and she ann in your arms and may your will always be done.

Lord, help me ...

to give my all to you. I want to completly.

I am thankful for:

Keeping me safe my childrens and all of the gifts you gave me.

Date: March 5, 2020

Prayer should be the key of the day and the lock of the night. ~ George Herbert

A — ADORATION

My praise to God:

Sue - That I came to visit
Shan - That He showed a way
for me to able to come and
visit

C — CONFESSION

I ask God for forgiveness:

allowing negativity to destroy
your happiness.

T — THANKSGIVING

I am thankful for:

S — SUPPLICATION

Requests to God:

Sue - to show her a way that
she can slowly learn to lean
on God.

Date: March 8, 2022

Verse for today:

Whenever you are enveloped in
trials or fall into temptations
Be assured that the trial
and proving of your faith bring
out endurance & patience

Prayers for others:

To help them lean on
you in all that they do.

Lord, help me ...

To lean
completely
on you.

I am
thankful for:

God being grant
of my life
everyday.

Date: March 9, 2022

Prayer – secret, fervent, believing prayer – lies at
the root of all personal godliness. ~ William Carey

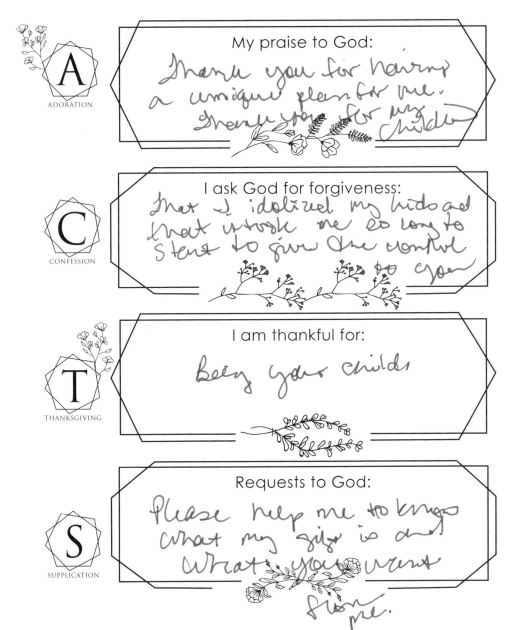

A ADORATION

My praise to God:

Thank you for having a unique plan for me. Thank you for my children

C CONFESSION

I ask God for forgiveness:

That I idolized my kids and that it took me so long to start to give the control to you

T THANKSGIVING

I am thankful for:

Being your childs

S SUPPLICATION

Requests to God:

Please help me to know what my gift is and what you want from me.

Date: March 9, 2022

Verse for today:

No one has ever seen God, but if we love one another, God lives in us

Prayers for others:

I pray for my daughters safety and that you walk with them, guide them, and help heal their hearts

Lord, help me ...

w/ keeping my cool when dealing w/ my ex and know you will help me.

I am thankful for:

you, God. If it wasn't for you I would be lost.

Date: March 10, 2022

If you only pray when you're in trouble, you're in trouble.

A — ADORATION

My praise to God:

Making sure that I have a way to thrive

C — CONFESSION

I ask God for forgiveness:

My impure thoughts and nasty dreams

T — THANKSGIVING

I am thankful for:

all of the many gifts you give me

S — SUPPLICATION

Requests to God:

Please help me w/ my medical journey

his medical class

Date:

Verse for today:

Prayers for others:

Lord, help me ...

I am
thankful for:

Date: _____

If life gets too hard to stand ... kneel.

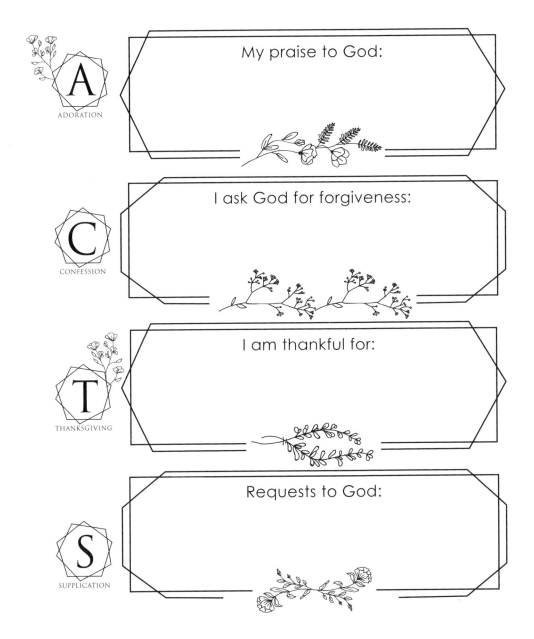

A — ADORATION

My praise to God:

C — CONFESSION

I ask God for forgiveness:

T — THANKSGIVING

I am thankful for:

S — SUPPLICATION

Requests to God:

Date:

Verse for today:

Prayers for others:

Lord, help me ...

I am thankful for:

Date: _____

Fervent prayers produce phenomenal results.

A — ADORATION

My praise to God:

C — CONFESSION

I ask God for forgiveness:

T — THANKSGIVING

I am thankful for:

S — SUPPLICATION

Requests to God:

Date:

Verse for today:

Prayers for others:

Lord, help me ...

I am
thankful for:

Date: _____

Don't forget to pray today, because God didn't forget to wake you up this morning.

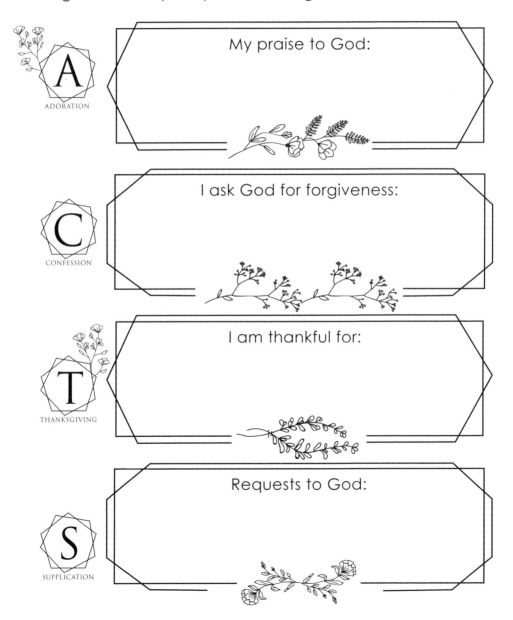

A
ADORATION

My praise to God:

C
CONFESSION

I ask God for forgiveness:

T
THANKSGIVING

I am thankful for:

S
SUPPLICATION

Requests to God:

Date:

Verse for today:

Prayers for others:

Lord, help me ...

I am
thankful for:

Date: _____

When you can't put your prayer into words, God hears your heart.

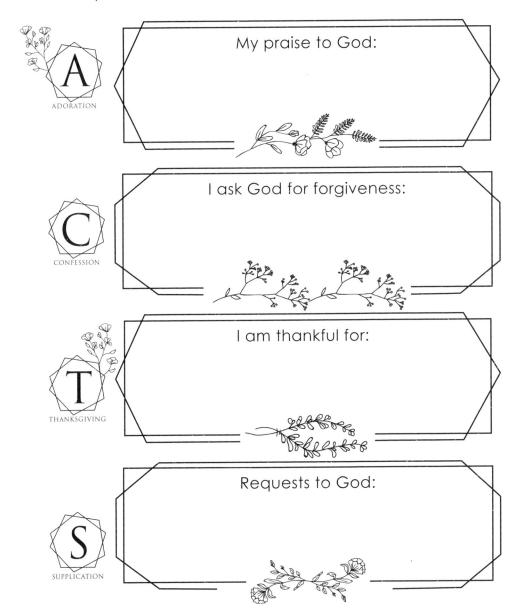

A ADORATION

My praise to God:

C CONFESSION

I ask God for forgiveness:

T THANKSGIVING

I am thankful for:

S SUPPLICATION

Requests to God:

Date:

Verse for today:

Prayers for others:

Lord, help me ...

I am
thankful for:

Date: _____

I do believe in the power of prayer.

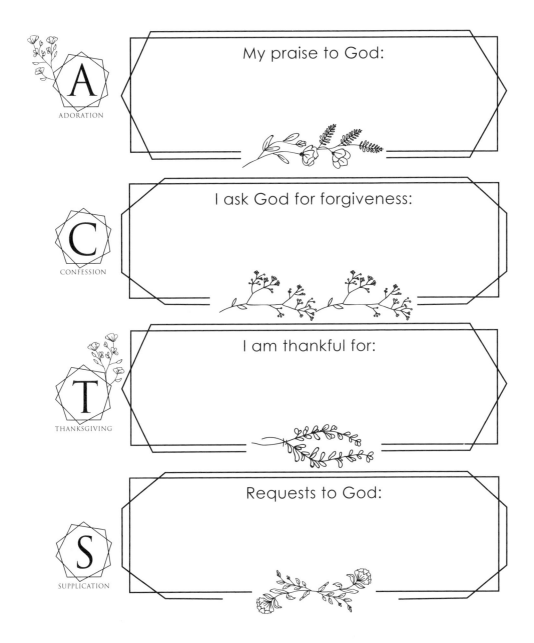

A — ADORATION

My praise to God:

C — CONFESSION

I ask God for forgiveness:

T — THANKSGIVING

I am thankful for:

S — SUPPLICATION

Requests to God:

Date:

Verse for today:

Prayers for others:

Lord, help me ...

I am
thankful for:

Date: _____

Prayer does not fit us for the greater work: it is the greater work. ~ Oswald Chambers

A
ADORATION

My praise to God:

C
CONFESSION

I ask God for forgiveness:

T
THANKSGIVING

I am thankful for:

S
SUPPLICATION

Requests to God:

Date:

Verse for today:

Prayers for others:

Lord, help me ...

I am thankful for:

Date: _____

When life is tough pray, when life is great pray.

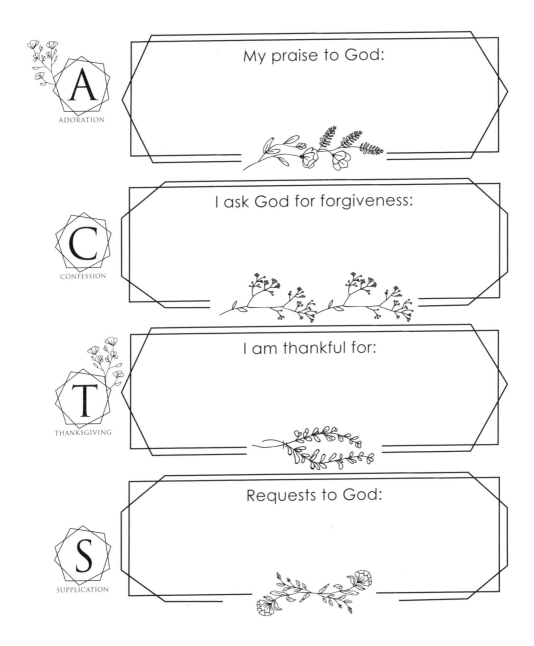

A ADORATION

My praise to God:

C CONFESSION

I ask God for forgiveness:

T THANKSGIVING

I am thankful for:

S SUPPLICATION

Requests to God:

Date:

Verse for today:

Prayers for others:

Lord, help me ...

I am
thankful for:

Date: _____

Is prayer your steering wheel or your spare tire?
~ Corrie ten Boom

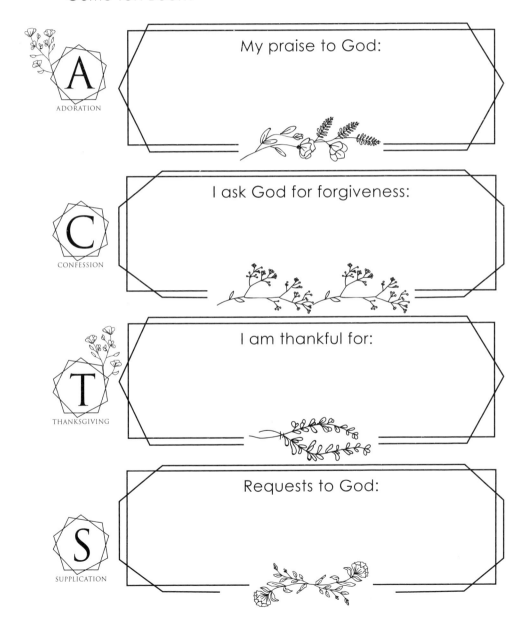

A ADORATION

My praise to God:

C CONFESSION

I ask God for forgiveness:

T THANKSGIVING

I am thankful for:

S SUPPLICATION

Requests to God:

Date:

Verse for today:

Prayers for others:

Lord, help me ...

I am
thankful for:

Date: _____

Prayer is the nearest approach to God.
~ William Law

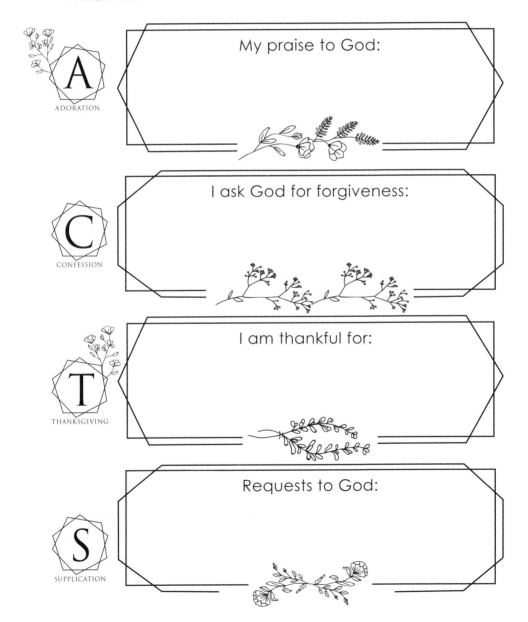

A — ADORATION

My praise to God:

C — CONFESSION

I ask God for forgiveness:

T — THANKSGIVING

I am thankful for:

S — SUPPLICATION

Requests to God:

Date:

Verse for today:

Prayers for others:

Lord, help me ...

I am
thankful for:

Date: _____

Prayer is not so much an act as it is an attitude – an attitude of dependency, dependency upon God.
~ A. W. Pink

A
ADORATION

My praise to God:

C
CONFESSION

I ask God for forgiveness:

T
THANKSGIVING

I am thankful for:

S
SUPPLICATION

Requests to God:

Date:

Verse for today:

Prayers for others:

Lord, help me ...

I am
thankful for:

Date: _____

If the only prayer you ever say is "thank you,"
it will be enough. ~ Meister Eckhart

A ADORATION

My praise to God:

C CONFESSION

I ask God for forgiveness:

T THANKSGIVING

I am thankful for:

S SUPPLICATION

Requests to God:

Date:

Verse for today:

Prayers for others:

Lord, help me ...

I am
thankful for:

Date: _____

Work as if you were to live a hundred years, pray as if you were to die tomorrow. ~ Benjamin Franklin

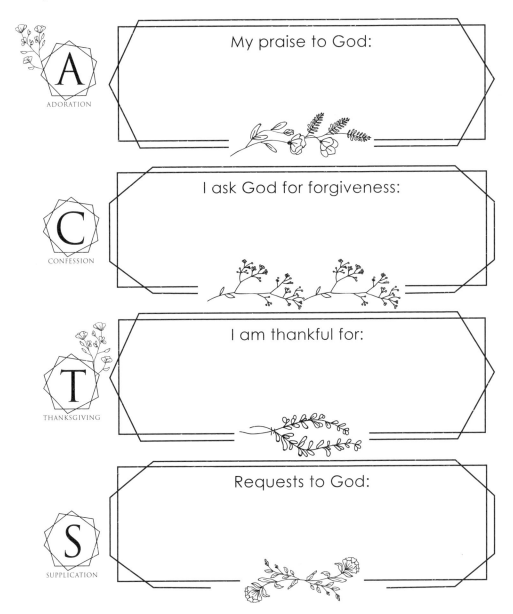

A ADORATION

My praise to God:

C CONFESSION

I ask God for forgiveness:

T THANKSGIVING

I am thankful for:

S SUPPLICATION

Requests to God:

Date: _____

Verse for today:

Prayers for others:

Lord, help me ...

I am
thankful for:

Date: _____

Prayer is the exercise of drawing on the grace of God. ~ Oswald Chambers

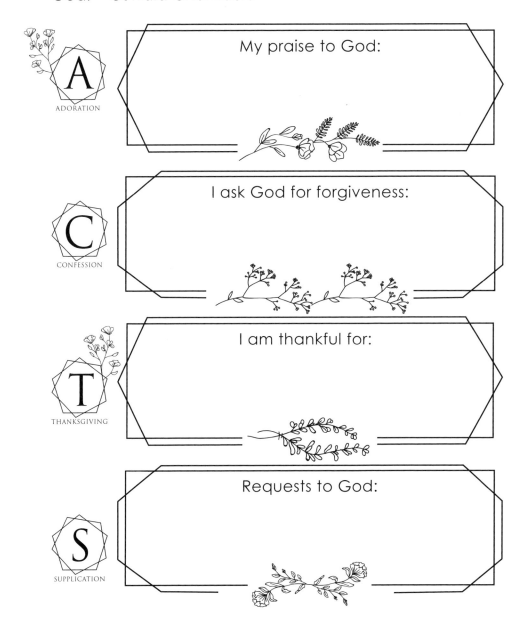

A — ADORATION
My praise to God:

C — CONFESSION
I ask God for forgiveness:

T — THANKSGIVING
I am thankful for:

S — SUPPLICATION
Requests to God:

Date:

Verse for today:

Prayers for others:

Lord, help me ...

I am
thankful for:

Date: _____

Never doubt the power of prayer.

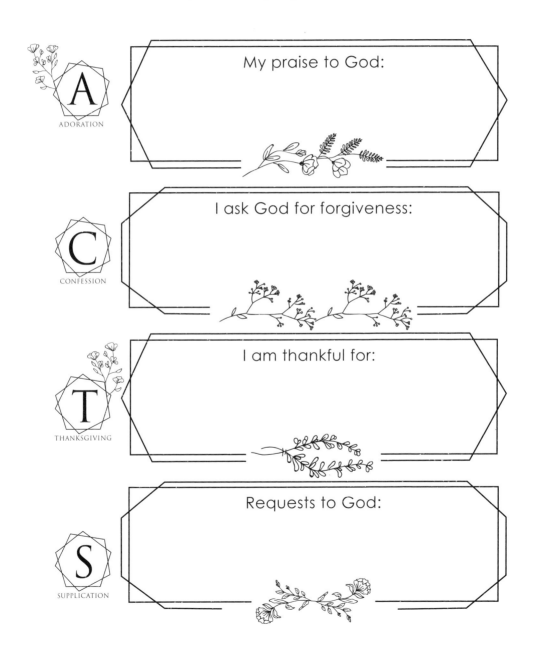

A ADORATION

My praise to God:

C CONFESSION

I ask God for forgiveness:

T THANKSGIVING

I am thankful for:

S SUPPLICATION

Requests to God:

Date:

Verse for today:

Prayers for others:

Lord, help me ...

I am
thankful for:

Date: _____

Prayer changes everything.

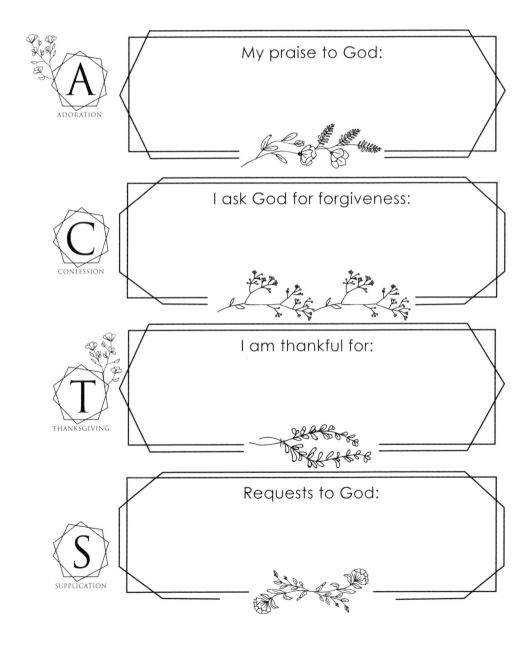

A
ADORATION

My praise to God:

C
CONFESSION

I ask God for forgiveness:

T
THANKSGIVING

I am thankful for:

S
SUPPLICATION

Requests to God:

Date: _____

Verse for today:

Prayers for others:

Lord, help me ...

I am
thankful for:

Date: _____

God speaks in the silence of the heart. Listening is
the beginning of prayer. ~ Mother Teresa

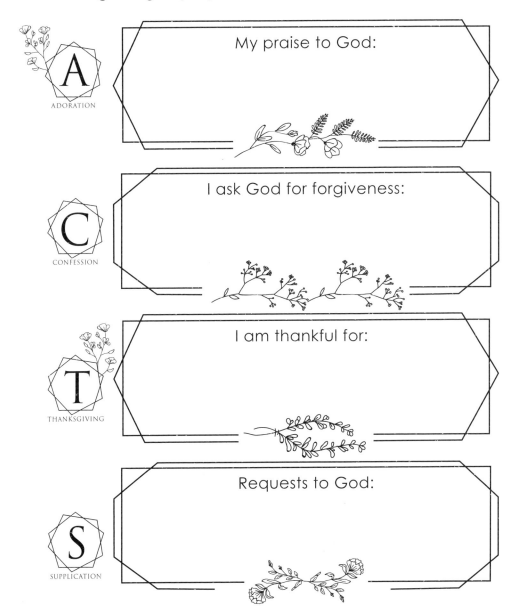

A — ADORATION

My praise to God:

C — CONFESSION

I ask God for forgiveness:

T — THANKSGIVING

I am thankful for:

S — SUPPLICATION

Requests to God:

Date:

Verse for today:

Prayers for others:

Lord, help me ...

I am
thankful for:

Date: _____

Jesus is just a prayer away. ~ Greg Laurie

A ADORATION

My praise to God:

C CONFESSION

I ask God for forgiveness:

T THANKSGIVING

I am thankful for:

S SUPPLICATION

Requests to God:

Date:

Verse for today:

Prayers for others:

Lord, help me ...

I am
thankful for:

Date: _____

The person who prays grows. ~ F. B. Meyer

A — ADORATION

My praise to God:

C — CONFESSION

I ask God for forgiveness:

T — THANKSGIVING

I am thankful for:

S — SUPPLICATION

Requests to God:

Date:

Verse for today:

Prayers for others:

Lord, help me ...

I am
thankful for:

Date: _____

Sometimes all it takes is just one prayer to change everything.

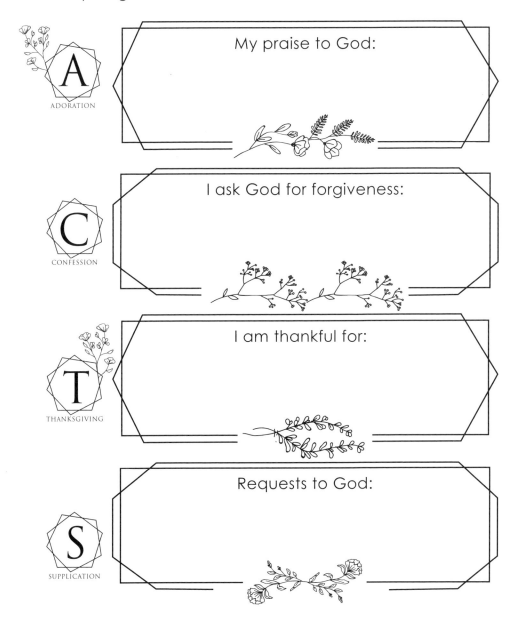

A ADORATION

My praise to God:

C CONFESSION

I ask God for forgiveness:

T THANKSGIVING

I am thankful for:

S SUPPLICATION

Requests to God:

Date:

Verse for today:

Prayers for others:

Lord, help me ...

I am
thankful for:

Date: _____

Prayers go up, blessings come down.

A
ADORATION

My praise to God:

C
CONFESSION

I ask God for forgiveness:

T
THANKSGIVING

I am thankful for:

S
SUPPLICATION

Requests to God:

Date:

Verse for today:

Prayers for others:

Lord, help me ...

I am
thankful for:

Date: _____

Time spent in prayer is never wasted.
~ Francois Fenelon

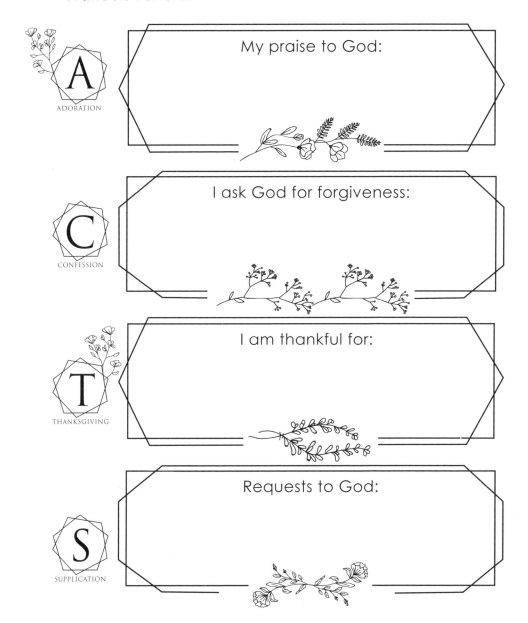

A
ADORATION

My praise to God:

C
CONFESSION

I ask God for forgiveness:

T
THANKSGIVING

I am thankful for:

S
SUPPLICATION

Requests to God:

Date:

Verse for today:

Prayers for others:

Lord, help me ...

I am
thankful for:

Date: _____

Prayers outlive the lives of those who utter them;
outlive a generation, outlive an age, outlive a world.
~ E. M. Bounds

A ADORATION

My praise to God:

C CONFESSION

I ask God for forgiveness:

T THANKSGIVING

I am thankful for:

S SUPPLICATION

Requests to God:

Date: _____

Verse for today:

Prayers for others:

Lord, help me ...

I am
thankful for:

Date: _____

Our prayers do make a difference.
~ Max Lucado

A
ADORATION

My praise to God:

C
CONFESSION

I ask God for forgiveness:

T
THANKSGIVING

I am thankful for:

S
SUPPLICATION

Requests to God:

Date:

Verse for today:

Prayers for others:

Lord, help me ...

I am
thankful for:

Date: _____

Love the people who treat you right. Pray for those who don't. Life is too short to be anything but happy.

A ADORATION

My praise to God:

C CONFESSION

I ask God for forgiveness:

T THANKSGIVING

I am thankful for:

S SUPPLICATION

Requests to God:

Date: _____

Verse for today:

Prayers for others:

Lord, help me ...

I am thankful for:

Date: _____

No man is greater than his prayer life.
~ Leonard Ravenhill

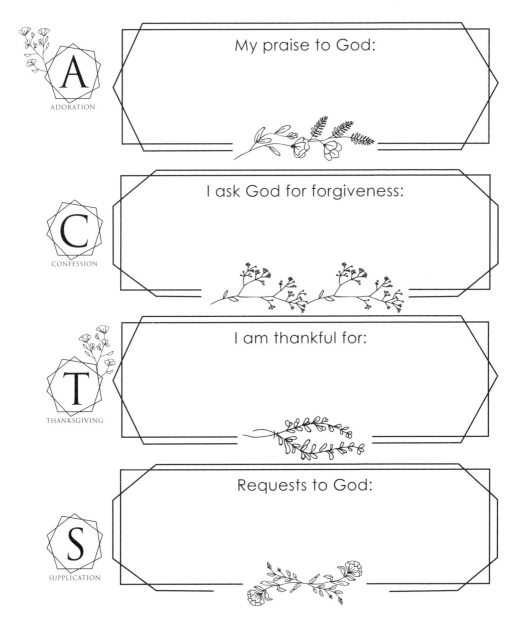

A ADORATION

My praise to God:

C CONFESSION

I ask God for forgiveness:

T THANKSGIVING

I am thankful for:

S SUPPLICATION

Requests to God:

Date:

Verse for today:

Prayers for others:

Lord, help me ...

I am
thankful for:

Date: _____

Prayer – the world's greatest wireless connection.

A
ADORATION

My praise to God:

C
CONFESSION

I ask God for forgiveness:

T
THANKSGIVING

I am thankful for:

S
SUPPLICATION

Requests to God:

Date:

Verse for today:

Prayers for others:

Lord, help me ...

I am
thankful for:

Date: _____

Prayer – the key to all the treasures of this life and the hereafter.

A ADORATION

My praise to God:

C CONFESSION

I ask God for forgiveness:

T THANKSGIVING

I am thankful for:

S SUPPLICATION

Requests to God:

Date:

Verse for today:

Prayers for others:

Lord, help me ...

I am
thankful for:

Date: _____

The things you take for granted someone else is praying for.

A ADORATION

My praise to God:

C CONFESSION

I ask God for forgiveness:

T THANKSGIVING

I am thankful for:

S SUPPLICATION

Requests to God:

Date:

Verse for today:

Prayers for others:

Lord, help me ...

I am
thankful for:

Date: _____

Sometimes all you need to do is pray.

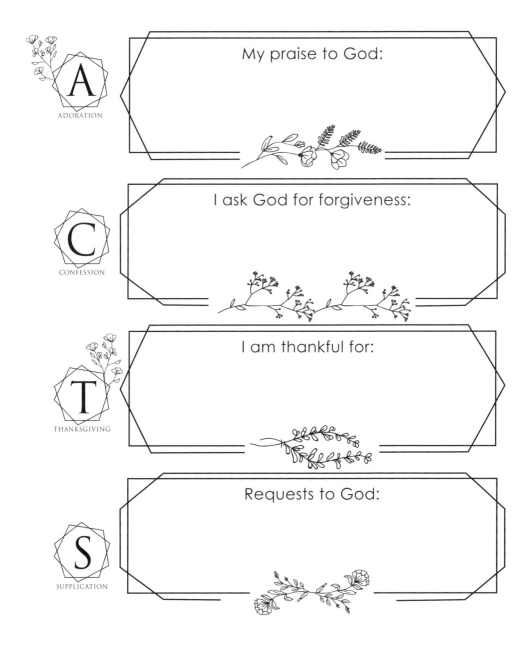

A ADORATION

My praise to God:

C CONFESSION

I ask God for forgiveness:

T THANKSGIVING

I am thankful for:

S SUPPLICATION

Requests to God:

Date: _____

Verse for today:

Prayers for others:

Lord, help me ...

I am
thankful for:

Date: _____

Don't think of the things you didn't get after praying.
Think of the countless blessings God gave you without asking.

A
ADORATION

My praise to God:

C
CONFESSION

I ask God for forgiveness:

T
THANKSGIVING

I am thankful for:

S
SUPPLICATION

Requests to God:

Date: _____

Verse for today:

Prayers for others:

Lord, help me ...

I am
thankful for:

Date: _____

Prayer is our greatest power.
~ W. Clement Stone

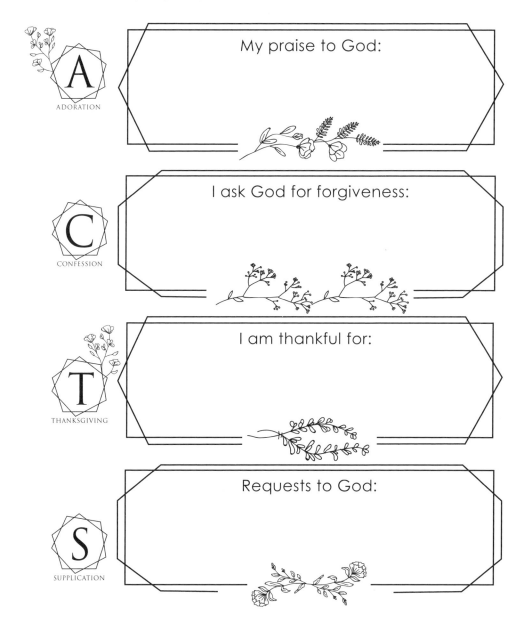

A
ADORATION

My praise to God:

C
CONFESSION

I ask God for forgiveness:

T
THANKSGIVING

I am thankful for:

S
SUPPLICATION

Requests to God:

Date: _____

Verse for today:

Prayers for others:

Lord, help me ...

I am
thankful for:

Date: _____

To be a Christian without prayer is no more possible than to be alive without breathing. ~ Martin Luther

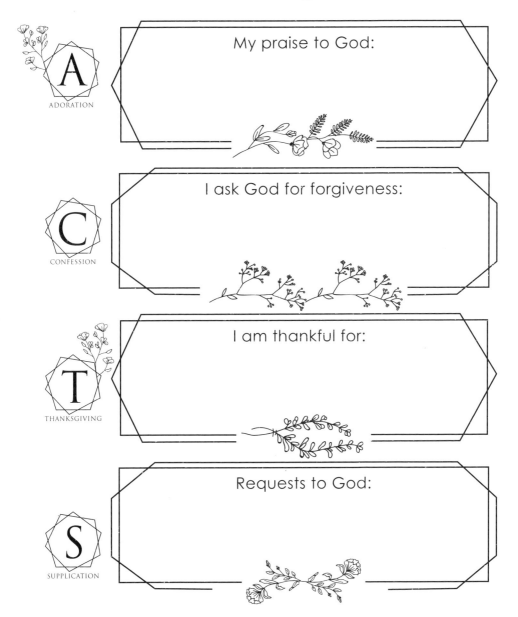

A — ADORATION

My praise to God:

C — CONFESSION

I ask God for forgiveness:

T — THANKSGIVING

I am thankful for:

S — SUPPLICATION

Requests to God:

Date:

Verse for today:

Prayers for others:

Lord, help me ...

I am
thankful for:

Date: _____

In prayer it is better to have a heart without words than words without a heart. ~ John Bunyan

A ADORATION

My praise to God:

C CONFESSION

I ask God for forgiveness:

T THANKSGIVING

I am thankful for:

S SUPPLICATION

Requests to God:

Date:

Verse for today:

Prayers for others:

Lord, help me ...

I am
thankful for:

Date: _____

There is no need to get to a place of prayer; pray wherever you are. ~ Oswald Chambers

A ADORATION

My praise to God:

C CONFESSION

I ask God for forgiveness:

T THANKSGIVING

I am thankful for:

S SUPPLICATION

Requests to God:

Date:

Verse for today:

Prayers for others:

Lord, help me ...

I am
thankful for:

Date: _____

It is not the body's posture, but the heart's attitude that counts when we pray. ~ Billy Graham

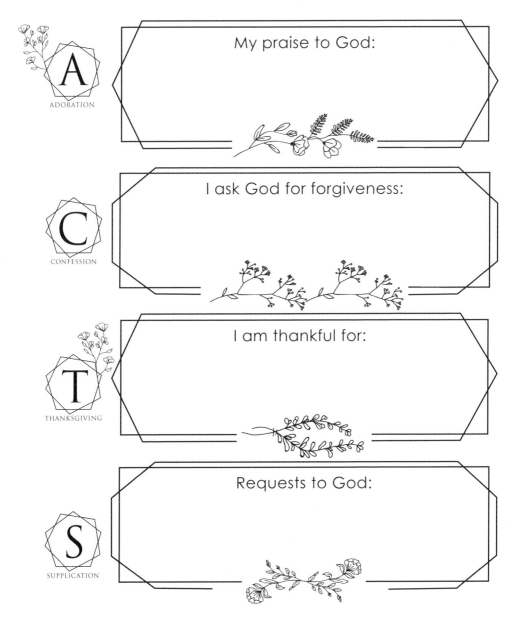

A
ADORATION

My praise to God:

C
CONFESSION

I ask God for forgiveness:

T
THANKSGIVING

I am thankful for:

S
SUPPLICATION

Requests to God:

Date:

Verse for today:

Prayers for others:

Lord, help me ...

I am
thankful for:

Date: _____

When you don't know what to pray or how to pray, take God's words and make them your prayers.

A — ADORATION

My praise to God:

C — CONFESSION

I ask God for forgiveness:

T — THANKSGIVING

I am thankful for:

S — SUPPLICATION

Requests to God:

Date:

Verse for today:

Prayers for others:

Lord, help me ...

I am
thankful for:

Date: _____

Prayer is an act of love; words are not needed.
All that is needed is the will to love. ~ St. Teresa of Avila

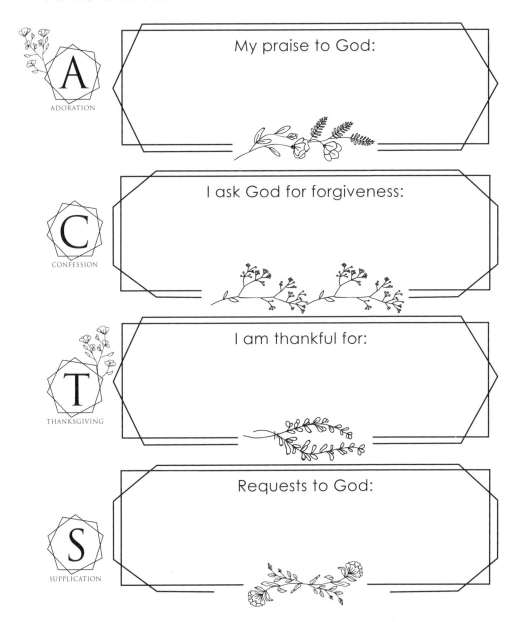

A ADORATION

My praise to God:

C CONFESSION

I ask God for forgiveness:

T THANKSGIVING

I am thankful for:

S SUPPLICATION

Requests to God:

Date:

Verse for today:

Prayers for others:

Lord, help me ...

I am
thankful for:

Date: _____

God shapes the world by prayer. The more praying there is in the world the better the world will be. ~ E. M. Bounds

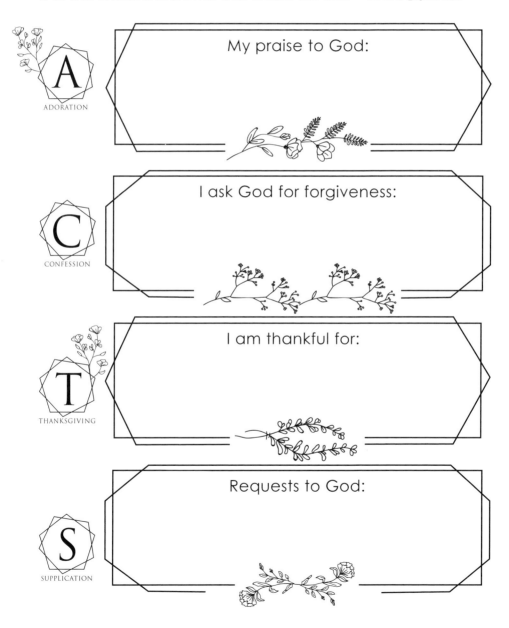

A ADORATION

My praise to God:

C CONFESSION

I ask God for forgiveness:

T THANKSGIVING

I am thankful for:

S SUPPLICATION

Requests to God:

Date:

Verse for today:

Prayers for others:

Lord, help me ...

I am
thankful for:

Date: _____

Do what you can and pray for what you cannot
yet do. ~ St. Augustine

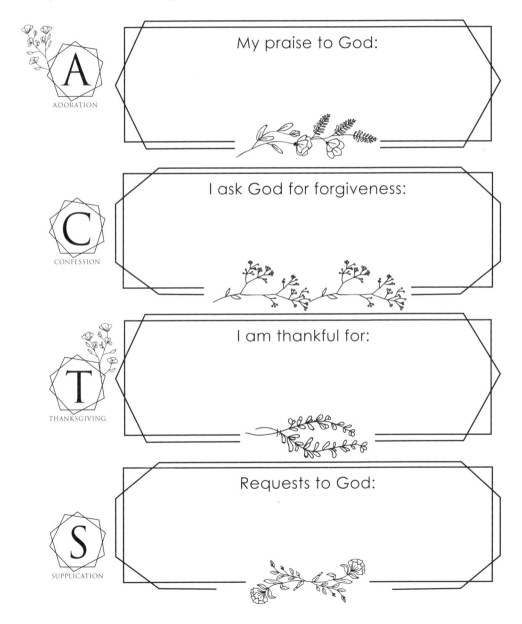

A ADORATION

My praise to God:

C CONFESSION

I ask God for forgiveness:

T THANKSGIVING

I am thankful for:

S SUPPLICATION

Requests to God:

Date:

Verse for today:

Prayers for others:

Lord, help me ...

I am
thankful for:

Date: _____

Prayer is a conversation with God, don't be afraid to tell Him what's on your heart.

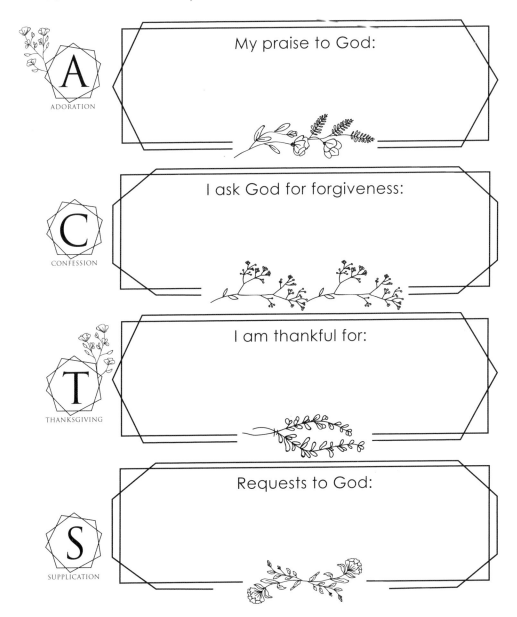

A ADORATION

My praise to God:

C CONFESSION

I ask God for forgiveness:

T THANKSGIVING

I am thankful for:

S SUPPLICATION

Requests to God:

Date:

Verse for today:

Prayers for others:

Lord, help me ...

I am
thankful for:

Date: _____

What blood is to the body, prayer is to the soul.
~ Mother Teresa

A
ADORATION

My praise to God:

C
CONFESSION

I ask God for forgiveness:

T
THANKSGIVING

I am thankful for:

S
SUPPLICATION

Requests to God:

Date:

Verse for today:

Prayers for others:

Lord, help me ...

I am
thankful for:

Date: _____

Any concern too small to be turned into a prayer is too small to be made into a burden. ~ Corrie ten Boom

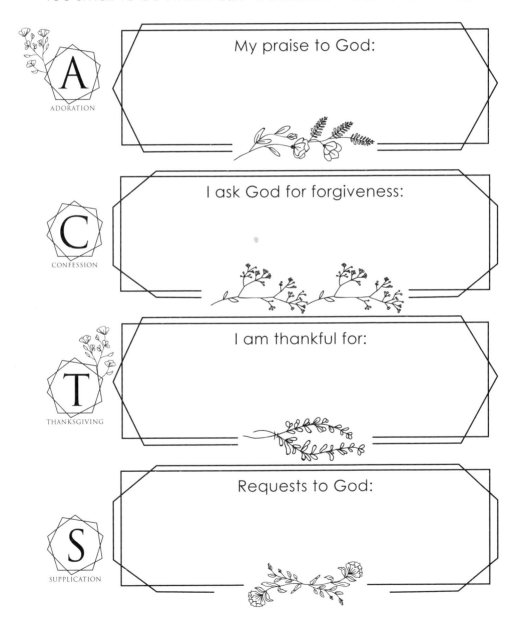

A
ADORATION

My praise to God:

C
CONFESSION

I ask God for forgiveness:

T
THANKSGIVING

I am thankful for:

S
SUPPLICATION

Requests to God:

Date:

Verse for today:

Prayers for others:

Lord, help me ...

I am
thankful for:

Date: _____

Prayer is the most concrete way to make our home in God. -- Henri Nouwen

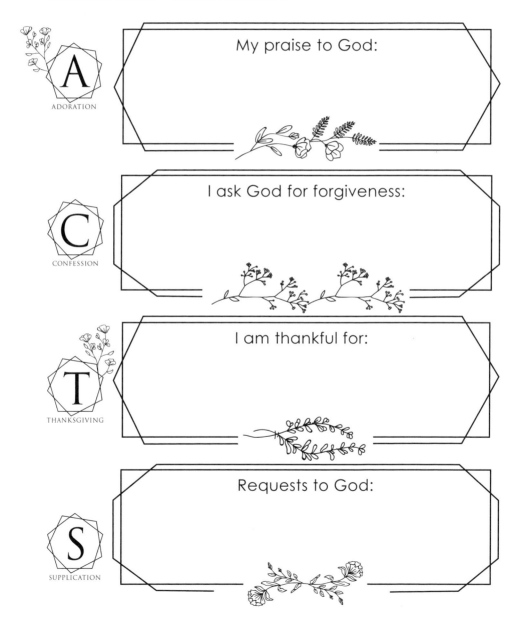

A ADORATION

My praise to God:

C CONFESSION

I ask God for forgiveness:

T THANKSGIVING

I am thankful for:

S SUPPLICATION

Requests to God:

Date:

Verse for today:

Prayers for others:

Lord, help me ...

I am
thankful for:

Date: _____

Our prayers have no expiration date. You never know when, where, or how God will answer.

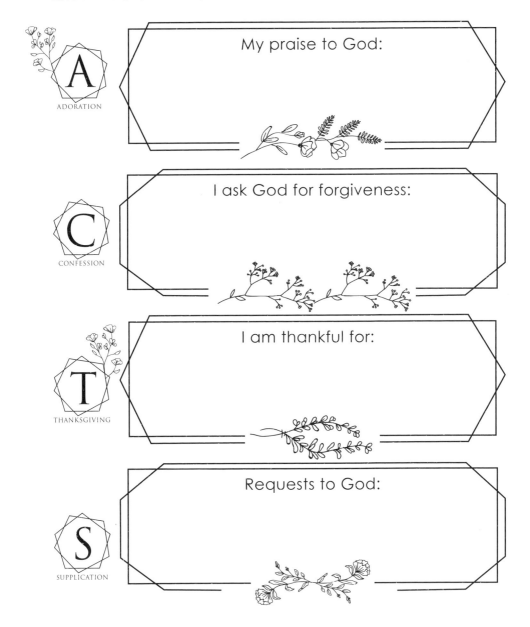

A
ADORATION

My praise to God:

C
CONFESSION

I ask God for forgiveness:

T
THANKSGIVING

I am thankful for:

S
SUPPLICATION

Requests to God:

Date:

Verse for today:

Prayers for others:

Lord, help me ...

I am
thankful for:

Date: _____

Our prayers are strengthened when we know God is listening and that He is faithful. ~ Dr. David Jeremiah

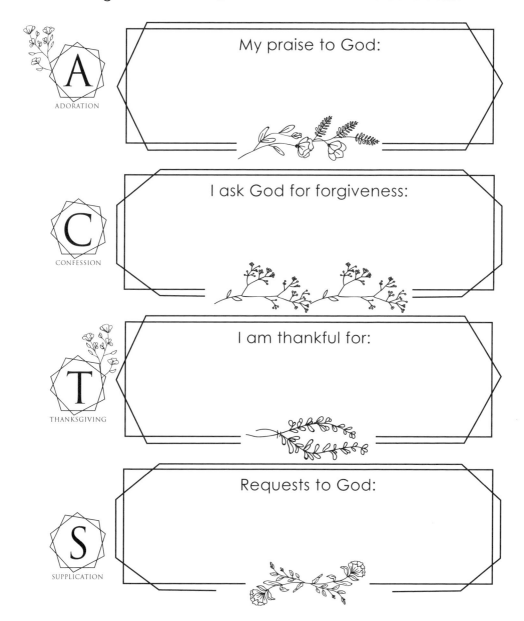

A ADORATION

My praise to God:

C CONFESSION

I ask God for forgiveness:

T THANKSGIVING

I am thankful for:

S SUPPLICATION

Requests to God:

Date:

Verse for today:

Prayers for others:

Lord, help me ...

I am
thankful for:

Date:

Prayer exercises your willpower and gives God authority to work in your life. ~ Max Lucado

A
ADORATION

My praise to God:

C
CONFESSION

I ask God for forgiveness:

T
THANKSGIVING

I am thankful for:

S
SUPPLICATION

Requests to God:

Date: _____

Verse for today:

Prayers for others:

Lord, help me ...

I am
thankful for:

Date: _____

Prayer honors God, acknowledges His being, exalts His
power, adores His providence, secures His aid. ~ E. M. Bounds

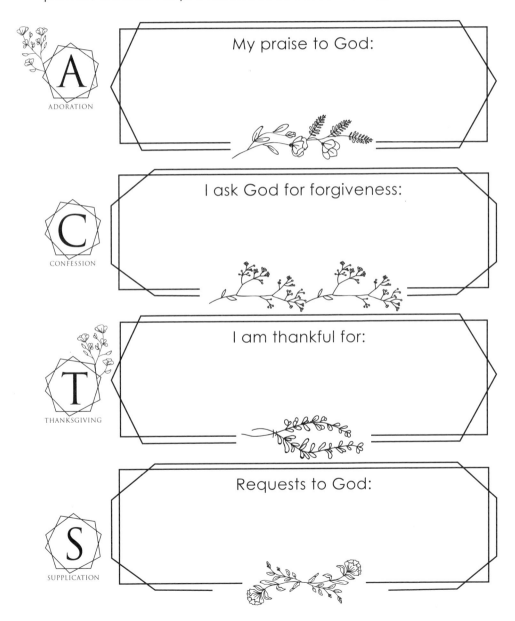

A
ADORATION

My praise to God:

C
CONFESSION

I ask God for forgiveness:

T
THANKSGIVING

I am thankful for:

S
SUPPLICATION

Requests to God:

Date: _____

Verse for today:

Prayers for others:

Lord, help me ...

I am
thankful for:

Date: _____

It is possible to move men, through God, by prayer alone. ~ Hudson Taylor

A — ADORATION

My praise to God:

C — CONFESSION

I ask God for forgiveness:

T — THANKSGIVING

I am thankful for:

S — SUPPLICATION

Requests to God:

Date: _____

Verse for today:

Prayers for others:

Lord, help me …

I am
thankful for:

Date: _____

The great people of the earth today are the people who pray, not those who talk about prayer. ~ S. D. Gordon

A ADORATION

My praise to God:

C CONFESSION

I ask God for forgiveness:

T THANKSGIVING

I am thankful for:

S SUPPLICATION

Requests to God:

Date: _____

Verse for today:

Prayers for others:

Lord, help me ...

I am
thankful for:

Date: _____

Don't stop praying. He hears you and He is working it out for your good.

A ADORATION

My praise to God:

C CONFESSION

I ask God for forgiveness:

T THANKSGIVING

I am thankful for:

S SUPPLICATION

Requests to God:

Date:

Verse for today:

Prayers for others:

Lord, help me ...

I am
thankful for:

Date: _____

We have to pray with our eyes on God, not on the difficulties. – Oswald Chambers

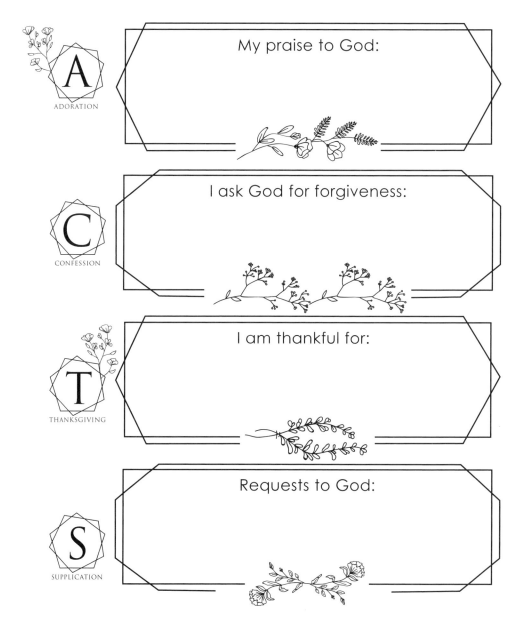

A ADORATION

My praise to God:

C CONFESSION

I ask God for forgiveness:

T THANKSGIVING

I am thankful for:

S SUPPLICATION

Requests to God:

Date:

Verse for today:

Prayers for others:

Lord, help me ...

I am
thankful for:

Date: _____

Prayer is as natural an expression of faith as breathing is of life. ~ Jonathan Edwards

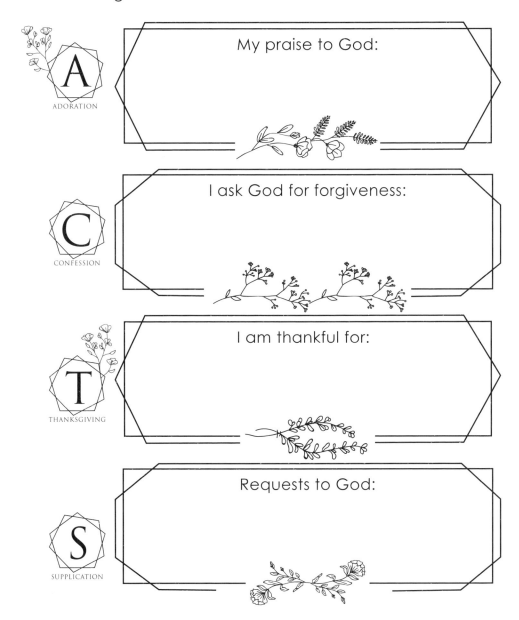

A — ADORATION

My praise to God:

C — CONFESSION

I ask God for forgiveness:

T — THANKSGIVING

I am thankful for:

S — SUPPLICATION

Requests to God:

Date:

Verse for today:

Prayers for others:

Lord, help me ...

I am
thankful for:

Date: _____

Prayer is the link that connects us with God.
~ A. B. Simpson

A ADORATION

My praise to God:

C CONFESSION

I ask God for forgiveness:

T THANKSGIVING

I am thankful for:

S SUPPLICATION

Requests to God:

Date:

Verse for today:

Prayers for others:

Lord, help me ...

I am
thankful for:

Date: _____

The ideal is for us to pray without ceasing. We should remain in a constant state of fellowship with the Father.

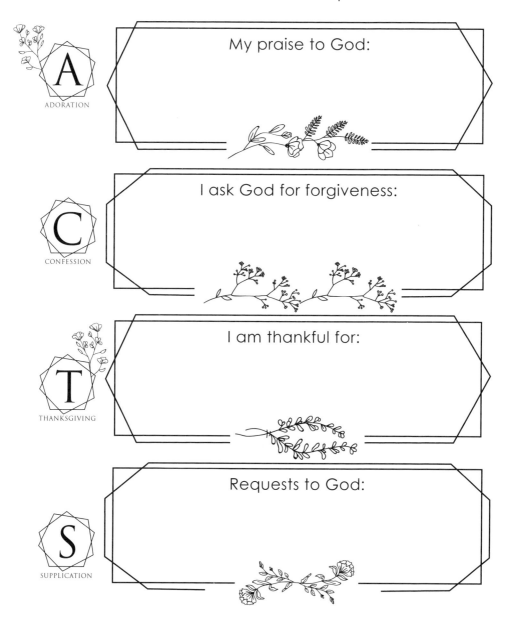

A ADORATION

My praise to God:

C CONFESSION

I ask God for forgiveness:

T THANKSGIVING

I am thankful for:

S SUPPLICATION

Requests to God:

Date:

Verse for today:

Prayers for others:

Lord, help me ...

I am
thankful for:

Date: _____

Prayer is simply a two-way conversation between you and God. ~ Billy Graham

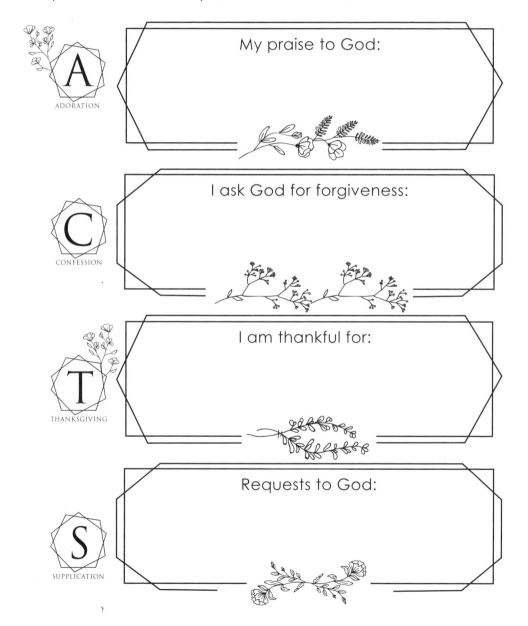

A ADORATION

My praise to God:

C CONFESSION

I ask God for forgiveness:

T THANKSGIVING

I am thankful for:

S SUPPLICATION

Requests to God:

Date:

Verse for today:

Prayers for others:

Lord, help me ...

I am
thankful for:

Date: _____

Today, as you pray, remember that God's timing is often different than ours.

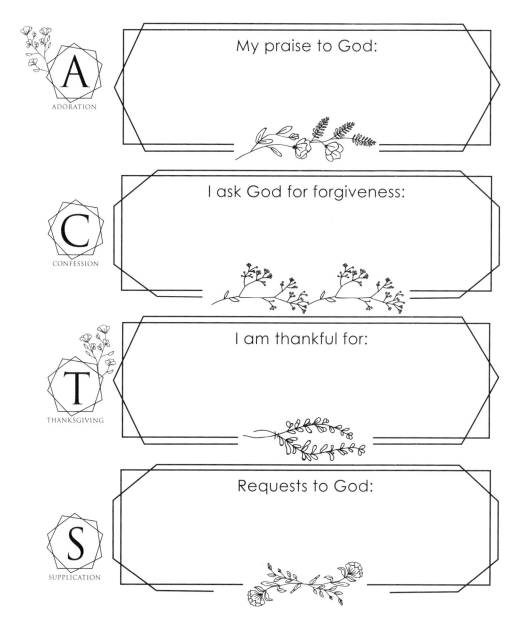

A
ADORATION

My praise to God:

C
CONFESSION

I ask God for forgiveness:

T
THANKSGIVING

I am thankful for:

S
SUPPLICATION

Requests to God:

Date:_____

Verse for today:

Prayers for others:

Lord, help me ...

I am
thankful for:

Date: _____

Pray as though everything depended on God. Work as though everything depended on you. ~ St. Augustine

A — ADORATION

My praise to God:

C — CONFESSION

I ask God for forgiveness:

T — THANKSGIVING

I am thankful for:

S — SUPPLICATION

Requests to God:

Date:

Verse for today:

Prayers for others:

Lord, help me ...

I am
thankful for:

⚜ CRISIS SCRIPTURE GUIDE ⚜

† **Anxiety**
Ps. 46:2-4
John 14:27
Phil. 4:6-8

† **Courage**
Josh. 1:9
Ps. 27:14
Hag. 2:4

† **Criticism**
Luke 6:37
Rom. 8:1
Rom. 8:34

† **Doubt**
Matt. 14:27-33
Matt. 21:21
James 1:6-8

† **Encouragement**
Ps. 23
John 16:33
James 1:2-4

† **Failure**
Ps. 145:14-16
Prov. 24:16-18
Hab. 3:17-18

† **Fear**
2 Tim. 1:7
1 John 4:18
Rev. 1:17-18

† **Forgiveness**
Matt. 6:14-15
Luke 11:4
Eph. 4:32

† **Freedom**
Isa. 61:1
John 8:31-36
Rom. 6:22

† **Gladness**
Neh. 8:10-11
Ps. 118:24
Phil. 4:4

† **Gossip**
Ps. 101:5
Prov. 18:8-9
Matt. 12:37

† **Honesty**
Ps. 32:2
Prov. 11:1-3
2 Cor. 4:2

† **Hope**
Rom. 5:2
1 Cor. 13:7
Col. 1:27

† **Joy**
Ps. 16:11
Ps. 112:1
Rom. 7:22

† **Loneliness**
Deut. 31:8
Ps. 23:4
John 14:18

† **Peace**
John 14:27
Phil. 4:6-7
Col. 3:15

† **Perseverance**
Matt. 10:22
Rom. 5:3-4
2 Pet. 1:5-7

† **Sorrow**
Isa. 25:8
Matt. 5:4
Rom. 12:15

† **Stress**
Ps. 9:10
Ps. 73:26
Ps. 91:7-11

† **Suffering**
Rom. 8:18-21
2 Cor. 4:8-9
1 Pet. 5:8-9

† **Uncertainty**
1 Cor. 9:26
Heb. 10:23
James 1:6-8